Hope Heals

A Journal of Love, Loss and Memories

by Sarah Kroenke and
Daena Esterbrooks

TRISTAN PUBLISHING

Minneapolis

Dedicated to children, teens and adults who have shared their
experiences of loss, courage and hope with us.
~Sarah and Daena

TRISTAN Publishing, Inc.
2355 Louisiana Avenue North
Golden Valley, MN 55427

ISBN 978-0-931674-65-5
First Printing
Printed in China

Hope Heals was made possible by the McCourtney family,
the Lou Newman family, Park Nicollet Foundation, Park Nicollet Methodist Hospice
and the Growing Through Grief program.

Special thanks to Nancy Gelle and Patti Betlach
for their contributions and support in publishing this book.

The Growing Through Grief program is a Minnesota based school
program designed to support children, teens and adults who are
grieving the death of a loved one.

Foreword

The most beautiful way to honor the relationship between you and your loved one is to grieve in a meaningful way. To acknowledge the love and memories shared, the pain of their absence and live a life that matters.

This journal was created out of an appreciation and understanding of how life changing and difficult it is to experience the death of a loved one. This journal is intended to be a safe place where you can be alone with your thoughts and memories. It can be a place where you share some of the most painful details of your loss. In doing so, we hope this journal can help guide you to rediscovering your "new normal" and provide renewed hope.

The journal does not have a specific beginning or end. It is designed so that you can work through your grief in a way that is most meaningful for you. Some of the pages have been left blank so you can do additional journaling, drawing or have a place to put photos of your loved one. You don't have to answer every question. You can choose to leave pages or portions of the pages blank. This journal is for you and you can decide where you want to start. It's okay to go back and revisit different parts of the journal at anytime. Just like grief, there are no rules.

We started using a similar journal in 1997 with teenagers and adults in group and individual grief counseling sessions. We found that many times what was most needed to heal and find a new normal was a dedicated place to write down details of a loved one's death, memories of their life, thoughts and feelings. This journal cannot take away the pain, but it can be used as a tool to discover growth and strength in the midst of the pain. The emotions expressed in this journal are more than just words or drawings they are a part of the healing process.

New paths await you in your heart and in your soul;
they just need to be discovered.
May you embrace the possibilities that life has to offer
and may you find peace.

Sarah Kroenke, BSSW, LSW & Daena Esterbrooks, MA, LPC

Dedicated to My Loved One

In loving memory of

_____
Who was born on

_____
And died on

_____
Today's date

_____

Who You Are and What You Mean to Me

I want to begin this journal by describing who you are and what you mean to me...

My Special Memories

Some of my special memories
& the times we shared together...

I Will Never Forget

the last time we were together or
spoke is a time I will never forget.
I remember...

If I could say or do one more thing
I would...

The Day My Life Changed

Date of your death _____

Time of your death _____

Location of your death _____

How I learned of your death...

How I felt...   What I did...

Your Memorial Service or Funeral

What was I thinking

Songs played or sung

What people said

Who was there

How I felt

What was the weather

What I wore

My Days, Weeks and Months

This is what my days, weeks
and months were like after your death

My Grief Has Changed Me

Dreams Irritability Lack of interest Headache

Lack of Sleep Hurtful thoughts Shorter attention span

Lack of Concentration Question faith Aggressive behavior

Pit in Stomach Preoccupied with death Mood swings

The Journey of Grief

Initial Grief

Shock / Disbelief / Emotionlessness

Angry / Guilty

Physical Symptoms
- headaches, stomach aches,
  sleeping difficulties, appetite changes

Anxiety / Fear

Hopeless with Grief

Anguish / Despair

Depression

Low motivation / Disinterest in normal activities

Vulnerable

Hopelessness

Exploration in Grief
Constant thoughts about death or loved one
Low self-esteem
Relationship conflicts
Looking to blame
Feelings of impatience / agitation
Searching for answers

Rebuilding Life
Small energy bursts
May struggle with fatigue / exhaustion
Trying to redefine / rediscover self
Reconnecting with old relationships / Forming new ones
Appreciation of what lies ahead

Living a New Normal
Creating / Discovering a new identity
without your loved one
Settling into a new routine
Acceptance and Peace
Genuine happiness
Hopeful

My New Normal

Ways my life has changed since your death...

Daytime Thoughts & Nighttime Dreams

Do you watch over me?

Do you miss me?

Are you protecting me?

What do you look like?

Do you communicate?

What do you say?

Where are you?

Are you at peace?

Remembering You

Your personality

Your hobbies and passions

The color of your eyes

Your favorite food

Your favorite TV show

Your favorite song

I will never forget

Memory Bracelet

The memories I have of you will be with me forever.

Think of memories that you have of your loved one
or memories you thought you would have.

Find beads that remind you of those memories.
String them together to make your bracelet. Once you
complete your bracelet you can record the meaning
of each bead on this page.

Bead (color or style) Memory

Forgiving and Believing

I can now forgive myself for...

I can now find peace in believing ...

Hoping and Knowing

My hopes are...

I know I will be okay because...

Coping

Time has revealed to me that
I have within myself the skills
I need to cope. Here are some
of the ways I have learned to cope.

Grieving is Healing: A Personal Reflection

the journey of healing hurts and is not easy.
It can be a slow, scary and confusing process.
Grieving is healing. If we don't grieve we don't heal.
Sometimes it might feel as if we will spend our whole
life healing, because healing is one step at a time.
It may seem like we take two steps forward and
one step back, but we are still moving. We are not
stuck in one place. Healing is giving grief our best
effort as we try to move forward.
Remember grieving is healing. If we don't grieve we
don't heal. the journey of healing hurts and is not
easy. We need to take it slow, take baby steps as we
move forward toward the challenges, towards the
future. Each step moving us closer to knowledge
and one step closer to healing. Because healing is
one step at a time.

Katie, age 13

Good-bye Letter

In writing this letter I realize
that good-bye is not forever because
I will always carry you in my heart.
Here is my good-bye letter to you.

Possibilities

It happened so gradually I barely
   stopped to notice.
The heaviness and heartache that
   once filled my chest has lightened.
My breathing has become easier
   because I've told your story
   and honored your memory.
The sound of your name no longer
brings me quickly to tears,
   but instead brings a gradual
   smile to my face.

The pain is still there, it is still
   very real, but that is okay.
I don't want to forget you,
   but instead just move forward
   with your memory in my heart.
What once felt so impossible, with
   time has become a possibility.

                              D.E.

Support & Self Care

These are the things that I do to take care of myself...

these are the places I go to for comfort...

these are the people I go to for support when I need to laugh, cry, talk or be listened to...

Honoring and Celebrating You

I will honor and celebrate you by...

What I would Say Today

If I could have a conversation today, I would tell you...

My Life Today

This is what I treasure about
my life today ...

What I Have Learned About Life

Because of your death, this is what
I have learned about life...

Tears Into Healing

First the tears come and you think they will never stop. And then, well, the tears continue. You start to believe that you may never see it or feel it, again...

Finally, one day it happens. A smile appears on your once tear-filled face and you feel hopeful, and a little guilty too. The smile is followed by laughter. It's a strange feeling, but it's good and you feel more alive than ever before.

You continue to grieve and remember. You smile, you laugh and you cry some more, but mixed in these tears is happiness.

Happiness in knowing that you had someone, so dear, to love. You move forward... appreciating the gifts of yesterday and the hopes of tomorrow... and you heal.
The healing and the love never stops.

S. K.

the following pages are a place for
you to write or draw your thoughts
and feelings as you remember your
loved one on special occasions ...
birthdays, holidays, anniversaries.
this is also a place where others
can write their memories or where
you can write memories that
others have shared with you .

More About Sarah and Daena

Sarah Kroenke, BSSW, LSW

Pain and healing...I have experienced them both. I've coped with many deaths in my life, the most significant being the death of my mother when I was a teenager. Being a motherless daughter for over 20 years has provided me sadness and challenges beyond words. However, because of my mother's death, I have been enriched with a deeper appreciation for love, life and all of its gifts.

Through my career, with Park Nicollet, as a hospice social worker and a counselor with Growing Through Grief I have had the privilege to witness the courage and power of the human spirits ability to transform suffering into strength. I am constantly reminded that just as grieving is a life-long process and an extension of love, so is healing. And, so we heal...

Daena Esterbrooks, MA, LPC

I have known the pain and heartache that death can bring. I remember so vividly how suffocating my grief, at times, would feel. I also remember the obstacles I faced as I began my own journey towards renewed hope and healing. But as I sit here today, over 6 years out from the death of my twin daughters, I am a stronger person for the experience. Because of my own grief journey I am a different mother to my daughter and a different counselor to the many students I work with.

As a counselor with the Park Nicollet Growing Through Grief program, I have one of the greatest jobs in the world. It is an honor and privilege to be invited into someone's life as they experience such raw heartache and pain and as they gradually rediscover hope and happiness in their lives. These are the people that have inspired us to create this book.